MOVING TOWARD MATURITY
BOOK 3

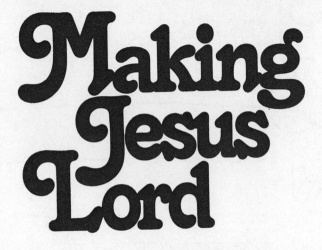

Making
Jesus
Lord

Barry
St. Clair

VICTOR BOOKS ®

A DIVISION OF SCRIPTURE PRESS PUBLICATIONS INC.
USA CANADA ENGLAND

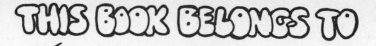

Produced in cooperation with REACH OUT MINISTRIES
120 N. Avondale Rd.
Avondale Estates, GA 30002

All Bible quotations, unless otherwise indicated, are from the *New International Version*, ©1973, 1978, 1984, International Bible Society. Used by permission of Zondervan Bible Publishers. Other quotations are from the *New American Standard Bible* (NASB), © the Lockman Foundation 1960, 1962, 1963, 1968, 1971, 1972, 1973, 1975, 1977; *The Living Bible* (TLB), ©1971, Tyndale House Publishers, Wheaton, IL 60189. Used by permission; and from the *King James Version* (KJV).

Sixth printing, 1988

Library of Congress Catalog Card Number: 83-51369

ISBN: 0-88207-303-6
© 1984, by Barry St. Clair. All rights reserved
Printed in the United States of America
For information, write to: VICTOR BOOKS, P.O. Box 1825, Wheaton, Illinois 60189.

CONTENTS

> "What you think about Jesus will determine who you are and how you behave."
>
> (A.W. Tozer)

SPECIAL THANKS

To Debbie Hayes for help in editing this manuscript.

To the Reach Out Ministries office staff for patiently working on this project.

To the youth ministers (especially the Reach Out Ministries team) from across the country who have tested this material and given valuable suggestions.

To my wife Carol and my children Scott, Katie, and Jonathan who have loved me and encouraged me to write this book.

To my mom and dad, who challenged me in my growing up years with the importance of God's Word and prayer.

To Buddy and Bev Price, my in-laws, whose prayer lives continue to be an inspiration to me.

And to the Lord Jesus Christ for teaching me who He is through spending time alone with Him.

Barry St. Clair

A WORD FROM THE AUTHOR

Jesus Christ has made positive changes in my life. He can change your life too. And He can use you to change others!

Just make yourself AVAILABLE, and Jesus can:

- ⇨ Help you know Him better.
- ⇨ Work in your life to make you a more mature Christian.
- ⇨ Motivate you to share Christ with others.
- ⇨ Use you to help other Christians grow toward maturity.
- ⇨ Make you a spiritual leader.

My goal for you is: "Just as you received Christ Jesus as Lord, continue to live in Him, rooted and built up in Him, strengthened in the faith as you were taught, and overflowing with thankfulness" (Colossians 2:6-7).

When that is happening in your life, then just as $2 \times 2 = 4$, and $4 \times 4 = 16$, and on to infinity, so Jesus can use you to multiply His life in others to make an impact on the world. How? One Christian (like you) leads another person to Christ and helps him grow to the point of maturity. That new Christian can lead another person to Christ and help him grow to maturity. And so the process continues. God gives you the tremendous privilege of knowing Him and making Him known to others. That is what your life and the Moving Toward Maturity series are all about.

The Moving Toward Maturity series includes five discipleship study books designed to help you grow in Christ and become a significant part of the multiplication process. For best results in your spiritual growth, begin with Book 1 and work your way through all five books. *Making Jesus Lord* is the third book in the series. The other books are:

Following Jesus (Book 1)
Spending Time Alone with God (Book 2)
Giving Away Your Faith (Book 4)
Growing On (Book 5)

God's desire and my prayer for you is that the things you discover on the following pages will become not just a part of your notes, but a part of your life. May all that's accomplished in your life be to His honor and glory.

Barry

PURPOSE

This book will help you discover why it is important to have Jesus as Lord. It will teach you to make decisions about making Jesus Lord in various areas of your life.

A disciple is a learner and a follower. As you learn to make Jesus Lord, you will learn about Jesus Christ and how to become more like Him. When that happens, you will be able to say with the Apostle Paul:

"We Christians have no veil over our faces; we can be mirrors that brightly reflect the glory of the Lord. And as the Spirit of the Lord works within us, we become more and more like Him" (2 Corinthians 3:18, TLB).

Before you begin doing the Bible studies in this book, make the commitment to let Jesus Christ bring to completion all He wants to do in your life. Remember: God cares more about what is being developed in your life than about what you write in this book.

USES FOR THIS BOOK

1. GROUP STUDY You can use this book as a member of an organized study group (Discipleship Family) led by an adult leader.* Each member of this group signs the commitment sheet, page 11, and agrees to use the book week by week for personal study and growth.

2. INDIVIDUAL STUDY You can go through this book on your own, doing one lesson each week for your own spiritual growth.

3. BUDDY STUDY You can ask a friend whc also wants to grow to join you in a weekly time of studying, sharing, and growing together.

4. ONE-ON-ONE DISCIPLESHIP After you have mastered and applied each Bible study in this book to your own life, you can help another person work through his or her own copy of the book.

*The Leader's Guide for *Making Jesus Lord* can be purchased at your local Christian bookstore or from the publisher.

PRACTICAL HINTS

(HOW TO GET THE MOST OUT OF THIS BOOK)

If you want to grow as a Christian, you must get specific with God and apply the Bible to your life. Sometimes that's hard, but this book can help you if you will:

1. Begin each Bible study with prayer.
Ask God to speak to you.

2. Use a study Bible.
Try the *New International Version* or the *New American Standard Bible*.

3. Work through the Bible study.
- ⇨ Look up the Bible verses.
- ⇨ Think through the answers.
- ⇨ Write the answers.
- ⇨ Jot down any questions that come up.
- ⇨ Memorize the assigned verse(s). (Use the Bible memory cards in the back of the book. Groups should select a single translation to memorize, in order to recite the verse(s) together.)

4. Keep a Time Alone with God Notebook.
During this study of *Making Jesus Lord*, you should continue to keep a record of your observations and insights. Your best option is to purchase a set of *Time Alone with God Notebook Inserts* at your local Christian bookstore, from the publisher or from Reach Out Ministries, and put them in a 5½" x 8½" loose-leaf notebook. Otherwise you will spend a lot of time making copies of daily forms, punching holes, and trying to keep a notebook up to date.

Each set of *Inserts* contains a 10-week supply of the forms you will need during your daily time with God. The *Inserts* can be used to accompany each book in the Moving Toward Maturity series or to continue your daily devotionals when you have completed the series. Your completed Time Alone with God Notebooks will become journals of your spiritual growth and encouragement as you look back and see how God has worked in your life.

5. Apply each Bible study to your life.

The main purpose of these studies is to discover how to make Jesus Lord. As you do:

↳ Ask God to show you how to act on what you're
↳ learning from His Word.
↳ Obey Him in your relationships, attitudes, and actions.
↳ Talk over the results with other Christians who
↳ can encourage and advise you.

IF YOU'RE IN A DISCIPLESHIP FAMILY

↳ *Before* each group meeting, set aside two separate times to work on the assigned Bible study. If possible, complete the whole Bible study during the first time. Then during the second time (the day of or the day before your group meeting), review what you've studied. This time should not be part of your time alone with God each morning. Do not use your time alone with God to work on your lesson.

↳ *After* you have discussed each Bible study with your Discipleship Family, complete the *Assignment* section of the study during the following week.

↳ Take your Bible, this book, your Time Alone with God Notebook, and a pen or pencil to every group meeting.

PERSONAL COMMITMENT

I, _____, hereby dedicate myself to the following commitments:

1. To submit myself daily to God and to all that He wants to teach me about growing as a Christian.

2. To attend all weekly group meetings, knowing that through my commitment I will not only have the best opportunity to grow, but that my very presence is an encouragement for the other members.

3. To complete the assignments without fail as they are due each week.

4. To be involved in my local church.

I understand that these commitments are not only to the Lord but to the group and to myself as well. I will do my very best, with God's help, to completely fulfill each one.

Signed _____

1

GET READY... GET SET!

Discovering Jesus' credentials

This was the first day of practice. At first I felt scared and kind of awkward. But Coach gave us a talk about being a team. You know, after we practiced for a while, it felt pretty good. But I've got a long way to go!

Can you recall the first day you started something new (a class, a sport, a musical instrument, etc.)? How did you feel?

_____

_____

Name one talent you have that you're really proud of.

_____

How long have you been doing it? How did you get to be good at it? Write a short paragraph that describes your learning process from the point you started until now.

_____

_____

_____

_____

_____

_____

Did you learn on your own, or did someone teach you?

Who contributed to your learning process?

_____

_____

COACHING CREDENTIALS

Having Jesus as Lord of your life is kind of like having a teacher or coach to help you be the best person you can be. What did Nicodemus say that Jesus was? (John 3:2)

_____

_____

Jesus Christ wants to teach you everything you need to know about being a Christian. But is He really qualified to do that? Let's look at His teaching credentials for being Lord of your life.

CREDENTIAL #1—HE CREATED YOU.
Read John 1:1-18 substituting "Jesus Christ" for "the Word" (Jesus is the Living Word of God). Compare that passage to Colossians 1:15-16 and describe how Jesus Christ was in on the creation of the world and, more specifically, *your* creation.

_____

Since Jesus created you, He knows how you work best. Read Psalm 139:13-16. What does Jesus Christ know about you?

_____

_____

Jesus Christ made you, and He knows all about you.

CREDENTIAL #2—HE IDENTIFIES WITH YOU.

Picture in your mind a story where the two main characters are a wicked leader (Evil Ruler) and a brave lad (Fearless Young Man). The people in the country where this story takes place have been starved, cheated, and oppressed by Evil Ruler. Fearless Young Man has grown up under Evil Ruler's reign and decides to save his people by overcoming Evil Ruler. If you want to know the end of the story, read John 1:14.

Jesus Christ came to earth as one of us. Through His death, He crushed Satan's rule on this earth forever. And because He lived here for 33 years, He knows what we go through every day. "We do not have a high priest (Jesus Christ) who is unable to sympathize with our weaknesses, but we have one who has been tempted in every way, just as we are" (Hebrews 4:15). Read Luke 4:1-13 and find out how Jesus faced the same temptations you have.

_____

_____

Jesus had struggles just like you have.

CREDENTIAL #3—HE REDEEMED YOU.

Redeemed means to "rescue." How did Jesus rescue you? (1 Corinthians 6:20; Romans 14:9)

_____

_____

Another definition for *redeem* is "to recover ownership by paying a specified sum," or "to ransom." If a gang kidnapped your best friend, how much would you pay

as a ransom to get him back? _____

_____

What ransom did Jesus pay for you? _____

_____

Jesus has paid to regain ownership of your life, so He has the right to be the Lord of your life. Jesus redeemed you at an expensive price.

JESUS' RESPONSIBILITIES AS LORD

"OK," you say, "I can see that Jesus is qualified to teach me and be Lord of my life, but what is a *lord* supposed to do anyway?" Three Greek words in the New Testament describe Jesus' role as Lord. Let's look at what each one means.

Despotes (master)—The meaning here is "unlimited power." Jesus can overcome anything when His unlimited power is in operation.

Basileus (monarch)—This word is more commonly used in the Orient to mean "all power and authority." A monarch's word is law. And because Jesus is God, He is always the truthful authority—the Boss.

Kurios (lord)—A lord, in this sense of the word, is the "owner." Wisdom and love are suggested in this word. Jesus as Lord is wise and loving.

Keep the meanings of these three words for *lord* in mind, and write your own definition of what it means for Jesus Christ to be Lord.

_____

_____

What does that definition mean to you personally?

_____

_____

MAKING IT PERSONAL

Jesus wants His lordship to become a reality in your life. How does that take place? As you go through this study of *Making Jesus Lord*, you will examine some very specific areas of your life: dating and sex, parents, attitudes, habits, thoughts, friendships, temptation, and material possessions. You will learn how the lordship of **17**

Jesus Christ affects each of those areas. But right now, you need to prepare! You can do two things to get ready to acknowledge Jesus as Lord of your life.

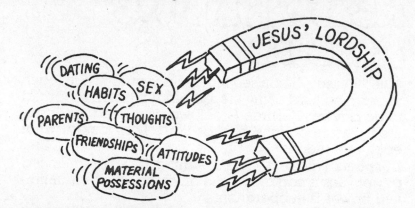

STEP #1: DESIRE.

The psalmist says, "O God, You are my God, earnestly I seek You; my soul thirsts for You, my body longs for You, in a dry and weary land where there is no water" (Psalm 63:1). This kind of desire comes when we get desperate! When we get tired of running our own lives, God will give us a desire to do it His way. Are you to the point where you are willing to let go and let God take over?

_____

The more we see who Jesus really is, the more the desire develops in us to please and worship Him. You will begin to see Jesus more clearly throughout the rest of _Making Jesus Lord._ But right now, evaluate where you stand as far as wanting Jesus to be the Lord of your life:

Are you tired of running your own life?_____Why?

_____

_____

What things do you know about Jesus that cause you to want to give yourself to Him as Lord?

_____

What doubts do you have about making Jesus the Lord of your life?

_____

_____

_____

Whatever your desires are at this moment, stop right now and pray that God would give you the desire to make Jesus the Lord of your life. Write your prayer here.

_____

_____

_____

_____

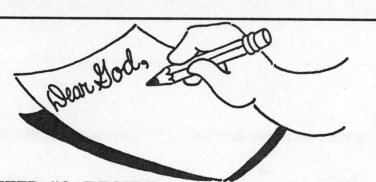

STEP #2: DECIDE.

When Paul realized on the road to Damascus who Jesus was, he said: "What shall I do, Lord?" Jesus told him: "Get up and go into Damascus. There you will be told all that you have been assigned to do" (Acts 22:10).

What did Paul do? He nailed down his commitment to make Jesus Lord right then and there. Look at his response: "I was not disobedient to the vision from heaven. First to those in Damascus, then to those in Jerusalem and all Judea, and to the Gentiles also, I preached that they should repent and turn to God and prove their repentance by their deeds" (Acts 26:19-20). You need to nail down your own commitment to making Jesus Lord of your life *right now.* Do it by faith, realizing that He will increase your desire for His lord-**19**

ship as time goes by. Silently, in your own words, let Jesus know that you have decided to make Him the Lord of your life. After you have committed to make Jesus your Lord, fill out the statement below.

Today, _____, I asked Jesus to be Lord of my life.
                Date

                    Signed: _____

Complete this Bible study by memorizing Psalm 63:1. (For tips on Scripture memorization, see page 4 in your *Time Alone with God Notebook Inserts.*)

ASSIGNMENT:

1. One of your assignments for this week (and through out this book) is to spend time alone with God every day. Each day you should read and study a short passage from the Gospel of Mark. This week, during your daily time alone with God, use the following Bible readings. Record your observations in a Time Alone with God Notebook. (*Time Alone with God Notebook Inserts* can be obtained from your local Christian bookstore, the publisher of this book, or Reach Out Ministries. These *Inserts* will provide practical advice for beginning or continuing a time alone with God. They also contain a 10-week supply of daily forms to keep your times with God going smoothly.)

   Day 1: Mark 1:1-11
   Day 2: Mark 1:12-13
   Day 3: Mark 1:14-15
   Day 4: Mark 1:16-20
   Day 5: Mark 1:21-34
   Day 6: Mark 1:35-38
   Day 7: Mark 1:39-45

2. Complete *Bible study 2*.

NOTES

2

NO PAIN, NO GAIN

Looking
at the
costs
and
benefits

Today the coach told me that I have the potential to be really good if I practice and get more rest (which means I'll have to get to bed earlier). I was really excited to hear that until I realized that I might have to give up hanging out with my friends after school and staying out late on school nights.

When you make Jesus Lord, you face some of these same choices. You have to lose something in order to gain something else. In this Bible study, you will take an honest look at the price you are willing to pay. On the other hand, you will also discover many benefits to having Jesus as Lord.

PAYING THE PRICE

Look up Matthew 16:24-26. Paraphrase these verses in your own words.

_____

_____

_____

Those are pretty strong words, aren't they? Let's take a closer look at what Jesus is really asking us to do.

COST #1—DENY YOURSELF

What does it mean to deny yourself? It means that you get rid of your "I, me, mine" approach to life—by making a sold-out commitment to Jesus Christ. The world teaches, "Look out for number one." But Jesus says to forget yourself because:

> ➪ He has taken over the responsibility of looking out for you. You don't have to worry about yourself.
> ➪ He wants to motivate you to be your very best for Him. You don't have to get hung up on yourself.

Name one specific way that you are still looking out for number one.

_____

_____

COST #2—TAKE UP YOUR CROSS.

Philippians 2:5-11 gives a good example of someone who took up His cross. How? Jesus took up His cross by becoming an obedient servant to His Father. How can you carry your cross?

_____

_____

> ➪ Have a willing attitude to give up anything that doesn't serve your Lord. Peter says that you have been given "everything (you) need for life and godliness" (2 Peter 1:3).

⇨ Be willing to endure suffering. What kind of suffering? The same kind of suffering you endure to get your body into shape. You must be willing to withstand some pressure (and even pain) to produce good results.

How should you respond to suffering? (James 1:2-4)

_____

_____

What does God promise to do when you suffer? (1 Peter 5:10)

_____

_____

What is the result of suffering for Christ? (Romans 8:17)

_____

_____

Cost #3—FOLLOW JESUS.

From your study of the first book of this series, *Following Jesus*, sum up what it means to follow Jesus.

_____

_____

When you follow Jesus you:
- ⇨ Enter a relationship with Him and become His companion
- ⇨ Go in the same direction as Jesus
- ⇨ Submit to His authority in your life
- ⇨ Obey Him now and in the future

GOOD DEALS

So there are costs if you want to make Jesus Lord. But there are good deals as well. Many times we ask: "What do I have to give up before I can be a follower of Jesus? Can I still smoke, drink, and mess around in the backseat of the car if I make Jesus my Lord?" A better question would be, "What activities do I have the privilege of giving up in order to follow Christ and get in on all of the good deals He has for me?"

Just as a sleek, fast car can really move with the right person behind the wheel, you can move down the road of life in the right direction with megahorsepower when Jesus is in your driver's seat. Having Him there allows you to live life at it's very best.

Here are some of the good deals Jesus has to offer:

GOOD DEAL #1—YOU WILL MAKE GOOD DECISIONS. Another way of saying "Jesus is Lord of my life" is to say "I am in the center of God's will for me." When you have decisions to make, God will give you specific guidance. Look up Proverbs 3:5-6. As you think of one big decision you are facing right now, how do these verses apply to your decision?

_____

GOOD DEAL #2—YOU WILL HAVE SATISFACTION. How do your mouth and body feel when you are really thirsty?

_____

Jesus is your spiritual thirst quencher. Read John 4:10-14. What does He say about Himself?

_____

_____

In what way do you need satisfaction right now?

_____

Jesus is "a river of life" flowing out of you. He satisfies your thirst for meaning in life.

GOOD DEAL #3—YOU WILL LEAD A VICTORIOUS LIFE. Examine what Paul says in 1 Corinthians 15:57: "But thanks be to God! He gives us the victory through our Lord Jesus Christ." Think of a time when you were victorious. How did it feel?

_____

_____

What victories are in store for those who make Jesus Lord? (Romans 5:17)

_____

GOOD DEAL #4—YOUR FUTURE HAS HOPE.
Lots of things make life tough these days: broken
homes, low grades, and people who hate you, to name
a few. Name one thing that is discouraging you.

_____

What does 2 Timothy 2:11-12 say will happen if you
hang in there?

_____

No matter how bad things look right now, you have a
bright future.

GOOD DEAL #5—YOUR CHARACTER WILL CHANGE.
Read Romans 8:28-29. Being "called according to His
purpose" is another way of saying "He is Lord of my
life." What will happen as a result of Jesus being your
Lord?

_____

_____

"Conformed to the likeness of His Son" means you will
begin to have His character qualities. What are some
of Jesus' qualities that you would like to develop?

_____

_____

_____

Reread Matthew 16:24-26. "Whoever wants to save his
life will lose it, but whoever loses his life for Me will save
it" (v. 25). By making Jesus Lord, you "lose your life" (so
to speak) because you turn everything over to Him. But
in doing so you gain real life and all of the positive
benefits that go along with it. Only then can you find
the life that God wants you to enjoy.

MAKING IT PERSONAL

Among the things you will have to lose in order to gain are your material possessions. What do you think of when you hear the word "materialism?" After checking a dictionary, write your definition here.

_____

_____

From now on, every Bible study session will conclude with a short Life Change sheet to help you apply God's truths to your own life. The following page contains a Life Change sheet dealing with the issue of materialism. Your part in making this lesson personal is to work through that sheet, thoroughly studying the Scripture passage and answering the questions that follow.

Complete this Bible study by memorizing Matthew 16:24.

ASSIGNMENT:

1. Have a time alone with God every day this week using the following Bible readings.
   Day 1: Mark 2:1-12
   Day 2: Mark 2:13-17
   Day 3: Mark 2:18-28
   Day 4: Mark 3:1-12
   Day 5: Mark 3:13-19
   Day 6: Mark 3:20-30
   Day 7: Mark 3:31-35

2. Complete *Bible study 3*.

LIFE CHANGE

ISSUE: Material Possessions
BIBLE STUDY: Matthew 6:19-34
(Use the Bible study method suggested on page 3 of your *Time Alone with God Notebook Inserts* on this and future Life Change sheets.) Use the space below to record your comments.

_____

_____

_____

_____

_____

_____

_____

_____

My weaknesses in the area of material possessions are:

_____

_____

_____

My strengths in the area of material possessions are:

_____

_____

_____

ACTION POINT
Based on my study of Matthew 6:19-34, I need to make Jesus Lord of my material possessions by:

_____

_____

_____

I will take the following specific step of action to begin to overcome the grip of material possessions of my life:

_____

_____

_____ will pray with me about this.

NOTES

3

WHAT'S THE DIFFERENCE?

**Experiencing Jesus'
greatness**

Today the coach said, "80 percent of the people in the world don't know what's happening, 15 percent watch what's happening, and 5 percent make things happen." I really want to be part of that 5 percent, but I'm not sure where to start.

Have you ever thought about the difference between someone who is successful and someone who is not? Name someone you know who is really successful.

_____

How do you think that person became successful?

_____

_____

The people who succeed in life make a decision somewhere along the way to become somebody special. Making Jesus Lord means that you have chosen to become someone special because Jesus is special. Why is He so special? For starters, He is God.

When the Bible refers to God, He might be called the Father, the Son (Jesus) or the Holy Spirit. God is three persons in one, and one person in three. That's kind of mind boggling, isn't it?

The word to describe all three persons of God is the Trinity, or Godhead. Let's look at some illustrations to get a rough understanding of the Trinity.

Each side of this triangle is equal, but distinct from the other two sides. Like a person can be a father, son, and husband at the same time, God has three identities in one.

Or imagine you are taking your SAT and see the following question. What would your answer be?
Which of the following has the chemical compound H_2O?
(A) Water
(B) Steam
(C) Ice
(D) All of the above.

You science majors would select D without a blink. You know that H_2O is a chemical compound with three different forms. This is a beautiful mystery. Ice is no more and no less H_2O than water or steam, yet the three compounds look quite different. In a similar manner, God reveals Himself in different ways, yet the Father, the Son, and the Holy Spirit are equal parts of the one God.

WHAT IS GOD LIKE?

If you really want to know what a person is like, you don't just look at his outward appearance. You look deeper inside to see what kind of *character* he has. Is he dependable? Honest? Loving? If he is a loving son, he will be a loving husband and a loving father.

God is like that. His character as the Father, Son, and Holy Spirit is the same—just expressed differently. Let's look at some of His qualities in order to begin to grasp what He is like.

QUALITY #1—GOD IS GREAT.

Take a map of the world and spend several minutes pinpointing and listing some of the countries you have never seen. Then find your state. How big is it compared to some of the countries you have never even seen?

God created the universe. Our galaxy is only one of many, many galaxies contained in the universe that God made. Our solar system is one of many in our galaxy. Planet Earth is one of the planets in our solar system. So your state is a small part of a country on a continent that is a small part of a planet in a galaxy that is only a small part of the universe that God created. Get the picture? Here's how Psalm 145:3 says it: "Great is the Lord and most worthy of praise; His greatness no one can fathom." Look at Isaiah 40 and list some of the ways God is great.

verse 12 _____

verses 15-17 _____

verses 21-22 _____

verse 23 _____

verses 25-26 _____

QUALITY #2—GOD IS CONSISTENT.

He never changes. You could pull out some of your grammar school pictures to see how you have changed. But your changes haven't all been physical. Sure you're a lot taller and stronger than you used to be. But you're probably a lot more mature as well. List a few ways you are more mature now than when you were in grade school.

_____

_____

_____

But God never changes. He can't mature the way we do because He is already perfect. He told Moses, "I am

39

who I am" (Exodus 3:14) which means, "I am the self-existent One who never changes." Take a closer look at some of God's consistencies.

His truth is consistent. Think of a time when you said something you wanted to take back. Then read Psalm 119:89; Isaiah 40:8; 45:23; and John 14:6. What do those verses tell you about God's truth?

_____

_____

His purpose is consistent. Read Numbers 23:19 and Hebrews 7:21. Why is it that God never needs to reverse His plans?

_____

_____

QUALITY 3—GOD IS HOLY.

A.W. Tozer said, "Holy is the way God is. To be holy He does not conform to a standard. He is that standard. He is absolutely holy with an infinite, incomprehensible fullness of purity that is incapable of being other than it is" (*The Knowledge of the Holy,* Harper and Row). That is quite a statement. Rephrase it in your own words.

_____

_____

Read and study Isaiah 6:1-8. Based on that passage, what do you think holiness is?

_____

_____

How did Isaiah respond to God's holiness?

_____

_____

What does God want us to be? _____

Why? _____

To be "holy" means to be set apart." You are set apart because you belong to God. Romans 6:11 and Ephesians 2:1-6 tell you who you are set apart *for* and what you have been set apart *from*.

I am set apart *for* _____

I am set apart *from* _____

How did God set you apart from sin?

_____

_____

_____

BEING SET APART

Ephesians 4 describes some practical ways in which you can be holy. Paul begins the chapter with the word "Therefore," so it's important to know what he was saying *before.* The passage you just read (Ephesians 2:1-6) sums up what Paul's "therefore" refers to. Paul is saying that because you have died to sin and are alive to God, you *can* become holy by putting off your old (sinful) nature and putting on the new (godly) one. Study the following chart and Ephesians 4:25—5:8 to see where you need to put off your old personality and put on your new personality in Christ.

MAKING THE CHANGE

From	To	Because
Falsehood	Truthfulness	We're all members of one body
Wrong Anger	Controlled anger	You should not give the devil a foothold
Stealing	Useful labor	You can share with those in need
Unwholesome talk	Words that build others up	You can benefit those who listen

Bitterness and rage	Kindness and compassion	You should not grieve the Holy Spirit
Brawling and Slander	Forgiveness	Jesus forgave you
Sexual immorality, impurity, and greed	Love	You are holy
Obscenity, foolish talk and coarse joking	Thanksgiving	Because you are the light of God

Complete this Bible study by memorizing 1 Peter 1:15-16.

MAKING IT PERSONAL

Perhaps you see several areas listed above that you feel you need to improve in your life. That's OK. But a common problem that young people face is the next to the last category: "Sexual immorality, impurity, and greed." Specifically, how is your dating life? At the end of this session is another Life Change sheet—like the one you did last week on materialism. Right now, complete the questions for this week's Life Change issue: Sex and Dating.

ASSIGNMENT:
1. Have a time alone with God every day using the following Bible readings:
   Day 1: Mark 4:1-12
   Day 2: Mark 4:13-20
   Day 3: Mark 4:21-34
   Day 4: Mark 4:35-41
   Day 5: Mark 5:1-20
   Day 6: Mark 5:21-43
   Day 7: Mark 6:1-6

2. Complete Bible study 4.

LIFE CHANGE

ISSUE: Sex and Dating
BIBLE STUDY: 2 Corinthians 6:14—7:1
1 Thessalonians 4:3-8
Use the space below to record your comments.

_____

_____

_____

_____

_____

_____

_____

_____

My weaknesses in the area of sex and dating are:

_____

_____

_____

My strengths in the area of sex and dating are:

_____

_____

_____

ACTION POINT
Based on my study of 2 Corinthians 6:14—7:1 and
1 Thessalonians 4:3-8, I need to make Jesus Lord in my
sex and dating life by:

_____

_____

_____

I will take the following specific step of action to insure that I keep my dating and sex life within God's standards:

_____

_____

_____ will pray with me about this.

NOTES

4

TOTAL CONFIDENCE

Growing in faith

> The coach said today that if I can develop more confidence, I can probably make the first team. But how can I become more confident? I want to be the best I can be!

What does it take to reach your full potential in a sport?

_____

_____

What does it take to reach your full potential as a Christian?

_____

_____

The two questions above might have a lot of the same answers (practice, obedience, etc.). But another big prerequisite for living to your full potential is faith—believing that you can. Jesus Christ has great plans for you. Look at Jeremiah 29:11 and write down what He tells you about those plans.

_____

_____

In God's eyes, you are a person of great value. How important does God think you are? (Matthew 10:29-31)

_____

_____

GOD'S FAITHFULNESS

You recognize the value of your life when you begin to exercise your faith and understand Jesus' plans for you. But how can you develop that kind of faith? The first step is to try to understand God better, because God is the source of faith.

> Praise the Lord, all you nations;
> extol Him, all you peoples.
> For great is His love toward us,
> and the faithfulness of the Lord endures forever.
> Praise the Lord.
>
> (Psalm 117)

God's faithfulness causes His love and mercy to continue towards you. What does Lamentations 3:22-23 reveal about God's faithfulness toward you?

_____

_____

The two words "never fail" describe God's faithfulness.

Study the following verses and list some things that God is faithful to do in your life.

1 Corinthians 1:9 _____

1 Corinthians 10:13 _____

2 Thessalonians 3:3 _____

1 John 1:9 _____

God's faithfulness *to* us should inspire faith *in* us. Let's say you really need some help in algebra, and a fellow student offers to meet you after school and help you. If he didn't show up, how would you feel?

_____

_____

If he missed two or three appointments, would you keep trying to meet with him? _____
But if he made it to every meeting and helped you, wouldn't you begin to think, *Hey, here's someone I can count on*? Faith in God develops in the same way. God proves to you that He can be trusted, and you begin to have faith in Him.

How has God proven Himself trustworthy to you? Give a specific example.

_____

_____

How can you give Him additional opportunities to prove Himself faithful?

_____

_____

When God says He will do something, He *always* does it. And because God is faithful, you can develop faith in Him.

OUR FAITH

What is the biblical definition of faith? (Hebrews 11:1)

_____

_____

> Faith is confidence in your mind, your feelings, and your actions that God will come through.

An example of what faith is not—A man walks across Niagara Falls on a tightrope. People applaud. He walks across it again with a wheelbarrow. People get really excited. Do those people have faith that the tightrope walker knows what he is doing? You might think so. But suppose the guy asks for a volunteer to go across the Falls in his wheelbarrow. That is the test of how much the people believe in him. Genuine faith isn't sitting back and watching others. It is developed only when risk is involved.

An example of what faith is—When you sit down in a chair, do you worry about whether or not it will hold you up? Of course not. Why? Based on the evidence and your experience, a chair's purpose is to hold you up when you sit on it. As long as you're standing up, you are not expressing any faith. Faith comes when you sit down, relax, and put all your weight on the chair. Sitting down is one of many simple acts of faith we take every day. Everyone has faith in something. But what is really important is the *object* of your faith.

Jesus is the only object of your faith who will *never* let you down.

Let's take a closer look at what faith is.

FAITH IS CONFIDENCE.

Reread Hebrews 11:1. What do you think the following phrases refer to:

"what we hope for" _____

_____

"what we do not see" _____

_____

How can you "be sure" of such things?

_____

_____

FAITH IS BELIEVING IN YOUR MIND.

Read Hebrews 11:6. What are the two things you must believe intellectually in order to have faith?

_____

_____

What is God's response when you meet those requirements?

_____

_____

Abraham was known for his faith. Read Romans 4:18-21. What does it mean to be "fully persuaded"?

_____

_____

Are you fully persuaded that God can do what He promises? Why or why not?

_____

_____

FAITH IS ACTION.
Read Mark 11:24. According to that verse, how does faith become an action?

_____

_____

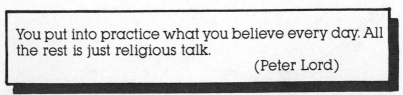

You put into practice what you believe every day. All the rest is just religious talk.

(Peter Lord)

Without action, faith does not exist. Faith is a *total* trust in God. He wants us to *act* on what we believe.

Through learning how to totally trust God, you can reach your maximum potential as a person and at the same time glorify Him. Look again at Romans 4:20-21. How can your potential and God's glory fit together according to these verses?

_____

_____

Now jot down one thought from each of the following verses on how you can reach your maximum potential and give glory to God through your life.

Romans 10:17 _____

Hebrews 11:8 _____

Hebrews 13:7 _____

1 Peter 1:6-7 _____

2 Peter 1:5-9 _____

INDICATION
OF
POTENTIAL

MAKING IT PERSONAL

One of the most important characteristics of a friendship is faithfulness—being able to be counted on. In order for a friendship to succeed, you need to trust the other person and have faith in him. To make this lesson on faith and faithfulness personal to your own life, work through the Life Change sheet on the issue of "Friendships." Think about how God's faithfulness and your faith can make you a better friend.

Complete this Bible study by memorizing Hebrews 11:1.

ASSIGNMENT:
1. Have a time alone with God every day this week using the following Bible readings.
   Day 1: Mark 6:7-13
   Day 2: Mark 6:14-29
   Day 3: Mark 6:30-44
   Day 4: Mark 6:45-52
   Day 5: Mark 6:53-56
   Day 6: Mark 7:1-23
   Day 7: Mark 7:24-30

2. Complete *Bible study 5.*

LIFE CHANGE

ISSUE: Friendships
BIBLE STUDY: 1 Samuel 18:1-5
Use the space below to record your comments.

_____

_____

_____

_____

_____

_____

_____

My weaknesses in the area of friendships are:

_____

_____

My strengths in this area of friendships are:

_____

_____

ACTION POINT
Based on my study of 1 Samuel 18:1-5, now I need to
make Jesus Lord of my friendships by:

_____

_____

I will take the following specific step of action to

strengthen my existing friendships and/or develop new ones.

_____

_____

_____ will pray with me about this.

NOTES

5

FOR REAL

Knowing the truth

> *I heard a rumor at school today that the coach didn't really play for the pros like he said he did. I really believed him when he talked about the "old days," but after today, I'm not sure who to believe.*

People talk about Jesus Christ in a lot of ways. You probably hear a lot of negative rumors about Him at school. Most of them probably aren't true, but they can stir up some doubts about His faithfulness. Let's look at some of the rumors about Jesus and then examine the proof so we can know for sure that Jesus was who He said He was.

PROOF POSITIVE

RUMOR #1—JESUS CHRIST WAS MERELY A GOOD TEACHER.

Proof #1—Jesus is more than just a good teacher. Only one person has ever fulfilled the Old Testament prophecies referring to the "Messiah"—Jesus Christ. Look up the following prophecies and see how they were fulfilled by Jesus.

PROPHECY	FULFILLMENT	WHAT HAPPENED?
Psalm 16:9-11	Acts 2:25-32	
Psalm 22:1	Matthew 27:46	
Psalm 34:20;	Matthew 27:35	
22:16-18	Luke 23:33	
	John 19:33-37	
Psalm 110:1	Acts 2:34-36	
	Hebrews 1:3	
Isaiah 53:7	Luke 23:8-9	
Isaiah 53:9	Luke 23:33, 50-53	

These are only a few examples. Jesus Christ fulfilled over 300 prophecies from the Old Testament. So He is obviously much more than a good teacher. In C.S. Lewis' classic book, *Mere Christianity* (MacMillan), he says: "A man who was merely a man and said the sort of things Jesus said wouldn't be a great moral teacher, he would either be a lunatic on the level with a man who says he is a poached egg, or else he would be the devil of Hell; you must make your choice.

"Either this was and is the Son of God, or else a madman or something worse. You can shut Him up for a demon, or you can fall at His feet and call Him Lord and God. But don't come up with any patronizing nonsense about His being a great moral teacher. He hasn't left that alternative open to us."

RUMOR #2—THE PROPHECIES THAT JESUS FULFILLED WERE WRITTEN DURING OR AFTER THE TIME OF JESUS.

Proof #2—In *Evidence That Demands a Verdict* (Here's Life), Josh McDowell points out that the Greek translation of the Hebrew Scriptures (known as the Septuagint) was completed by the year 250 B.C. So there had to be *at least* a 250 year gap between the written prophecies of Christ and their fulfillment. Read 2 Peter 1:20-21. What further proof does that passage provide regarding prophecies?

_____

_____

Evidence clearly indicates that Jesus was born many years after the prophecies about Him were written.

RUMOR #3—JESUS WASN'T REALLY GOD. HE WAS JUST A GREAT RELIGIOUS FIGURE.

Proof #3—Like C.S. Lewis said, no great religious figure would ever have made the claims Jesus made. What were some of Jesus' claims, and what evidence did He provide to prove He was telling the truth? Look up the following passages, and then decide if Jesus supported His claims to be God.

Claim	Evidence	Your Observations
John 6:35	John 6:1-14	
John 7:37	John 2:1-11	
John 8:12	John 9:1-25	
John 11:25-26	John 11:38-44	

Someone else believed Jesus' claims to be God—His Father. Read Matthew 3:16-17. What indications did God the Father provide to support Jesus' claims?

_____

_____

Other people believed Jesus was God. Read Matthew 14:25-32. What did those people say about Jesus?

_____

_____

RUMOR   #4—JESUS IS EQUAL TO MOHAMMED, CONFUCIUS, BUDDHA, AND OTHER GREAT RELIGIOUS LEADERS.

Proof #4—If you go to the graves of Mohammed, Confucius, or Buddha, you will find their bodies enshrined there. But that's not true of Jesus Christ. His grave is empty. Why? Because Jesus Christ was raised from the dead and ascended to heaven to be with the Father. Examine the following proof.

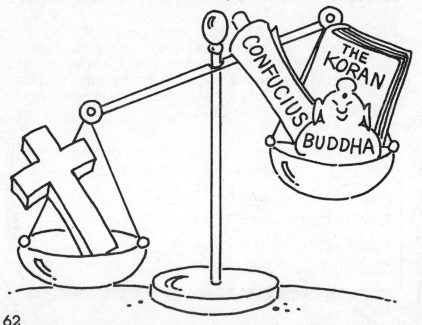

⤵ *Jesus prophesied His resurrection.* Rephrase Luke 18:31-34 in your own words.

_____

_____

_____

⤵ *Jesus' tomb was empty.* Read Matthew 27:57—28:7. What proof of Christ's resurrection do those verses provide?

_____

_____

⤵ *Jesus appeared to people after His death.* Read the following passages and make a list of those who saw Jesus alive after His death.

Matthew 28:1, 8-10 _____

Matthew 28:16-20 _____

Luke 24:13-16, 28-31 _____

Luke 24:34 _____

Luke 24:36-43 _____

John 20:14 _____

John 20:26-28 _____

John 21:1-14 _____

1 Corinthians 15:3-8 _____

Because of the proof of His resurrection, there can be *no* comparison of Jesus to other religious leaders.

RUMOR #5—JESUS WAS A JEW WHO DIED 2,000 YEARS AGO. HE DOESN'T HAVE ANYTHING TO DO WITH MY LIFE TODAY.

Proof #5—This proof is up to you. From your personal experience, how can you prove that Jesus is who He said He was and that He is still active today?

_____

_____

_____

_____

_____

TRUST AND OBEY

We can learn from the example that Christ has set for us. The one factor that allowed Jesus to be who He was and do what He did was His obedience to His Father.

↪ Jesus was obedient in baptism (Matthew 3:13-17).

↪ Jesus was obedient in every detail of His life (John 6:38).

↪ Jesus was obedient in death (Matthew 26:36-46).

Determine from the above passages what motivated Jesus to obey His Father.

_____

_____

Define obedience as you see it expressed through Jesus' life.

_____

_____

The greatest factor that will allow you to discover power and purpose in life is your obedience to God. When you make Jesus Lord, you become obedient to Jesus Christ and do what you know He wants you to do. And you experience some positive results of your obedience.

↪ You will be wise. Read Matthew 7:24-27 and rewrite this parable to apply to your own life.

_____

_____

⇨ You will experience God's love and fellowship. Look at John 14:23. What does that verse mean to you?

_____

_____

⇨ You will know Jesus better and better. Read John 14:21 to see how that happens.

_____

_____

⇨ You will be an overcomer. What promise does 1 John 5:3-4 hold for those who keep God's commandments?

_____

_____

Name one area of your life where it is really tough for you to be obedient to Jesus Christ.

_____

_____

Perhaps my toughest test of obedience happened while I was in college, playing basketball on a scholarship. One day while I was reading the Bible I came across Matthew 6:33: "Seek first His kingdom and His righteousness, and all these things (food, clothes, etc.) will be given to you as well." When I read that verse, I realized that playing basketball was more important to me than Jesus Christ. I struggled with the thought of *not* playing. I had played basketball since I was in first grade. The summer before my senior year in high school, I practiced eight hours a day—basketball was my life.

I didn't want to quit, but I kept thinking, *What comes first, basketball or Jesus Christ?* Finally one day my parents and I talked, cried, and prayed about my decision, and I knew that I needed to quit basketball.

After making that decision, I discovered how Jesus really takes care of us when we obey Him. I thought

that quitting basketball would leave a big void in my life. As soon as I quit, God put me in touch with a person who got me involved in working with students. Then a year and a half later, God gave me the opportunity to play for a basketball team that traveled all over the country playing major colleges and universities. But in addition to playing basketball, we shared our faith in Jesus Christ with the crowds of people who came to the games. I gave up basketball to seek Jesus first, and He gave basketball back to me.

MAKING IT PERSONAL

You probably know of several tough areas where you need to start being obedient to Jesus Christ. Let's take just one—your parents—and make it really personal to your life right now. Work through the Bible study on your Life Change sheet and then answer each question. Focus your thoughts on how your obedience to your parents will help you obey Jesus.

Complete this Bible study by memorizing John 14:21.

ASSIGNMENT:
1. Have a time alone with God every day this week using the following Bible readings:
   Day 1: Mark 7:31-37
   Day 2: Mark 8:1-13
   Day 3: Mark 8:14-21
   Day 4: Mark 8:22-26
   Day 5: Mark 8:27-30
   Day 6: Mark 8:31—9:1
   Day 7: Mark 9:2-13

2. Complete *Bible study 6.*

LIFE CHANGE

ISSUE: Obedience to parents
BIBLE STUDY: Ephesians 6:1-4; Colossians 3:20
Use the space below to record your comments.

_____

_____

_____

_____

_____

_____

_____

_____

My weaknesses in the area of obedience to parents are:

_____

_____

_____

My strengths in the area of obedience to parents are:

_____

_____

_____

ACTION POINT
Based on my study of Ephesians 6:1-4 and Colossians
3:20, I need to make Jesus Lord of my relationship with
my parents by:

_____

_____

_____

I will take the following specific step of action to become more obedient to my parents:

_____

_____

_____ will pray with me about this.

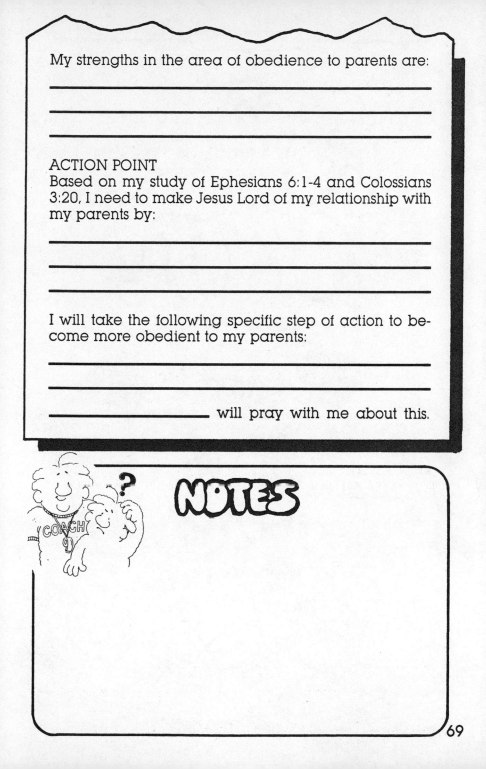

COACH

?

NOTES

6

GO FOR IT!

Changing your attitudes

Today during practice, one of the guys cussed me out because he got ticked off at me. I wanted to punch his lights out. It's hard to have the right attitude about people like him.

What would you do in a similar situation?

_____

_____

Why?

_____

_____

Your attitudes determine your actions just like your genes determine what you look like. I heard a story once that demonstrates the relationship between attitudes and actions. A guy named Steve Trass ran away from home and got a job in a lumber camp. He had lived a sheltered life and was kind of a sissy. One day he wrote home: "I hate this place. It's the worst place I've ever seen. The men are crude and nasty. I feel out of place."

But one night everyone in the camp went to town to get drunk—except for Steve. After the men had left, some guys from another lumber camp came to raid Steve's camp. Steve was scared and he didn't know what else to do, so he grabbed a nearby axe handle and turned out the light. As soon as the strangers came through the door, he started swinging. *Thud! Thud! Thud!*

Pretty soon the men from the other camp retreated. When Steve turned on the light, he saw seven bodies lying on the floor. That night he wrote home again: "I love this place. This is a place for men who are brave and strong. I am going to stay and make my fortune." This time he signed his letter "Your son, Axe Handle Trass." What a change of attitude!

ATTITUDE CHECK ✓

Do you recognize any of the following attitudes?
"I hate school."
"Gotta make my move on that girl!"
"My teacher came over on the *Mayflower!*"
"This stuff tastes like dog food."
"My parents have no right to tell me what to do."

If you are guilty of these thoughts (or worse), *you need a change of attitude.*

But don't exchange one bad attitude for another. You need to know what the right attitudes are. Jesus was a perfect example of someone with proper attitudes. Let's take a look at some of those attitudes and try to imitate them (as Paul challenges us to do in Philippians 2:5).

ATTITUDE #1—JESUS DIDN'T STRIVE FOR AMBITION AND SUCCESS.

He gave up His own desires and goals for His Father's desires and goals. Read Philippians 2:3. What two negative attitudes are named there?

How do you struggle with those attitudes?

_____

_____

What positive attitude should replace those negative ones?

_____

Philippians 2:6 describes how Jesus displayed that positive quality. Write what He did here.

_____

_____

Jesus "made Himself nothing." That means He poured out His own desires just like a glass of water. We need to pour out our attitudes of pride, selfishness, conceit, stubbornness, and defensiveness. Which of these attitudes do you need to get rid of?

_____

Emptying yourself may cost you your hopes, dreams, and desires.

ATTITUDE #2—JESUS GAVE UP HIS "RIGHTS" TO SERVE OTHERS.

What does Philippians 2:7 say about Jesus' "rights"?

_____

_____

What else can you learn about Jesus' attitude from Mark 10:45?

_____

_____

Many servants in Old Testament times were *hired*. They were paid wages and had certain rights. But the New Testament introduces the concept of a *bond* servant—someone who had no rights and was only the property of a master who could treat him however the master wished. Jesus was a *bond servant*. He voluntarily gave up His rights in order to glorify God and to serve men. If you look up Philippians 1:1 and 2 Corinthians 4:5 (in the *New American Standard Bible*), you will discover that the Apostle Paul called himself a bond servant. Who was his master?

People in our society think they have rights. Do you? Defend your answer.

_____

_____

How do you develop Jesus' servant attitude? By giving up your "rights." Since your last Life Change sheet was about parents, here are some practical ways to apply a servant attitude to your parents.

1. Look at life from your parents' perspective. How does your father feel about his job right now? His friends? His age? His relationship with your mom?

_____

_____

What about your mom? How does she feel about her life? Her feelings of self-worth? Your dad? Is she ever lonely?

_____

_____

2. Ask your parents' advice for problems you are facing. What do you need their advice about right now?

_____

_____

Name a recent bad decision you might not have made if you had consulted your parents first.

_____

_____

3. Show appreciation for your parents.

Here are some suggestions to get you started.

- ➪ take them out to dinner and *you* pay
- ➪ pick up your clothes
- ➪ clean up your room
- ➪ remember their birthdays and anniversary
- ➪ take out the trash
- ➪ vacuum the house

What will you do this week to show appreciation for your parents?

_____

_____

4. Pray for your parents. Make sure you remember your parents during your prayer times in your daily time alone with God. Use a "Record of Intercession" (pp. 15-20 in your *Time Alone with God Notebook Inserts*) and record your prayer requests for your parents.

5. Ask forgiveness from your parents when you do something wrong. Does tension

exist between you and your parents? Have you caused *any* of it? If so, you need to go to them and tell them you're sorry. Practice saying this out loud: "I was wrong. (Explain how.) Will you forgive me?" After you rehearse your apology several times, ask for your parents' forgiveness and record what happens.

_____

6. Tell your parents you love them. People are different. Your parents might respond positively, negatively, or indifferently when you say "I love you." But either way, it's important that they know you love them. (And don't just *say* it. *Show* it.) Their response can help you determine more specifically what to pray for them. Record their response here.

_____

_____

You can tell if you have a servant's attitude by the way you react when someone treats you like a servant.

ATTITUDE #3—JESUS GAVE UP HIS LIFE FOR DEATH ON THE CROSS. Read Philippians
2:8. Jesus struggled to be "obedient to death" in the Garden of Gethsemane (Matthew 26:38). The Bible pictures Jesus with "sweat . . . like drops of blood" as He was struggling to obey His Father. Read Matthew 26:39. Did Jesus want to die?

_____

Why did He decide to willingly give up His life?

_____

_____

You will never learn to live until you learn to die.

ATTITUDE #4—JESUS KNEW HE WOULD BE VICTORIOUS.
Read Philippians 2:9-11. What two things did God do as a result of Jesus' attitudes?

_____

_____

What two things should we do as a result of Jesus' attitudes?

_____

_____

What should we do to imitate Jesus' attitudes? (1 Peter 5:5-6)

_____

_____

You must go through the cross to get to the Resurrection.

Everything you do costs something (time, money, energy, etc.) The real question is whether or not you want to pay the price. If a football team wants to get to the state championship in December, they must practice in the sweltering heat of August. If a student wants to make the grades to get in one of the best colleges, he has to give up certain activities and study every night. If you want to set your sights on developing attitudes that will make you more like Christ, you must humble yourself before Jesus as Lord. Then His exciting promise is that He will exalt you, lift you up, and make you a winner in life.

MAKING IT PERSONAL

Are your attitudes like those that Jesus displayed? Or do you need "a change of attitude"? Your attitudes will determine your actions. To make this lesson personal, complete this session's Life Change sheet on "Attitudes," doing a Bible study of the passage of Scripture and then answering each question.

Complete this Bible study by memorizing Philippians 2:5.

ASSIGNMENT:
1. Have a time alone with God every day this week using the following Bible readings.
   Day 1: Mark 9:14-29
   Day 2: Mark 9:30-32
   Day 3: Mark 9:33-37
   Day 4: Mark 9:38-41
   Day 5: Mark 9:42-50
   Day 6: Mark 10:1-12
   Day 7: Mark 10:13-16
2. Complete *Bible study 7.*

LIFE CHANGE

ISSUE: Attitudes
BIBLE STUDY: Matthew 5:1-12.
Use the space below to record your comments.

_____

_____

_____

_____

_____

_____

_____

My weaknesses in the area of attitudes are:

_____

_____

_____

My strengths in the area of attitudes are:

_____

_____

_____

ACTION POINT
Based on my study of Matthew 5:1-12, I need to make
Jesus Lord of my attitudes by:

_____

_____

_____

I will take the following specific step of action to make
sure my attitudes reflect the lordship of Christ in my life:

_____

_____

_____ will pray with me about this.

NOTES

7

TURN HIM LOOSE

Living in the power of the Holy Spirit

I had a roommate in college who could be more than a little intimidating on the basketball court. I was a skinny six-foot guard, but he was a 6'4", 210-pound All-American. We used to play one-on-one. I would come back to the dorm room exhausted and humbled after spending much of our playing time with the ball stuffed down my throat.

My roommate would beat me time after time, and his victories began to take their toll as I began to lose my confidence. One afternoon, I was sitting in my room thinking about possible ways to defeat him. I fell asleep and the next thing I knew, I was dreaming that Kareem Abdul-Jabbar (probably the best basketball player who ever lived) was stuffed inside my body. I still looked like me on the outside, but inside I had become the best basketball player around.

The next day my roommate and I went to the gym to play our usual one-on-one. I decided to play it cool, so I dribbled the ball off my knee one time so he wouldn't suspect anything. But then I thought, *OK, Kareem baby, get loose!* I turned around and shot a perfect skyhook. It stripped the net. The next time I got the ball, I dribbled downcourt, put the move on my roommate, and slam dunked it right over his head. When he got the ball, I made him eat it . . . and I didn't even ask if he wanted salt and pepper on it. He never knew what hit him, because I obviously wasn't playing my normal game.

Have you ever wished you could be stronger than your normal self? When?

POWER FACTS

Jesus has given Christians an edge in the game of life. He has stuffed the person of the Holy Spirit right down inside them. What good does that do? Jesus said that "when He, the Spirit of truth, comes, He will guide you into all truth. He will not speak on His own; He will speak only what He hears, and He will tell you what is yet to come. He will bring glory to Me by taking from what is Mine and making it known to you" (John 16:13-14).

Having the Holy Spirit is like having "extra ability" as you face the test of living for Christ each day. Check out His promise to you in Ephesians 3:20-21: "Now to Him (Jesus) who is able to do immeasurably more than all we ask or imagine, according to His power (the Holy Spirit) that is at work within us, to Him be glory in the church and in Christ Jesus throughout all generations, for ever and ever!" The Holy Spirit gives you power to live the Christian life.

What do you really know about the Holy Spirit? Let's look at some of the "power facts" about Him.

POWER FACT #1—THE HOLY SPIRIT IS GOD.

He is the third person in the Trinity. Remember the diagram from *Bible study 3*?

Look up the following verses and record how they show that the Holy Spirit is God.

Matthew 28:19-20 _____

John 14:26 _____

1 Corinthians 12:13 _____

POWER FACT #2—THE HOLY SPIRIT HAS BEEN WORKING SINCE THE BEGINNING OF TIME.

How do the following verses confirm the Holy Spirit's early ministry?

Genesis 1:2 _____

Haggai 2:5 _____

POWER FACT #3—THE HOLY SPIRIT'S WORK WAS EVIDENT IN THE LIFE OF JESUS.

How do the following verses of Scripture verify the Spirit's work?

Luke 1:35 _____

Luke 4:1 _____

Luke 4:14-21 _____

John 1:32 _____

Romans 8:11 _____

Hebrews 9:14 _____

POWER FACT #4—THE HOLY SPIRIT INSPIRED THE BIBLE.

Read and summarize the following verses.

John 16:13 _____

_____

Acts 1:16 _____

_____

2 Peter 1:21 _____

_____

Does the fact that the Holy Spirit was the source of knowledge for all of the Bible writers give you more confidence in God's Word? Why?

_____

_____

POWER FACT #5—THE HOLY SPIRIT HELPS US TO BELIEVE IN CHRIST.

Read John 14:15-17. How does the Holy Spirit bring us to Christ?

_____

_____

Can unbelievers possess the Holy Spirit?

_____

_____

How can a non-Christian grieve the Holy Spirit? (Matthew 12:31-32)

_____

_____

POWER FACT #6—THE HOLY SPIRIT COMES TO LIVE INSIDE OF YOU.

What do the following verses reveal about a Christian's relationship with the Holy Spirit?

John 7:37-39 _____

1 Corinthians 12:13 _____

2 Corinthians 3:6 _____

Galatians 4:6 _____

Ephesians 1:13-14 _____

POWER FACT #7—THE HOLY SPIRIT CHANGES YOUR LIFE.

The following verses will help you see how the Holy Spirit living in you will make you more like Christ.

Ezekiel 36:26-27 _____

John 14:26 _____

Acts 1:8 _____

Romans 8:13-16 _____

1 Corinthians 12:4-11 _____

Galatians 5:22-23 _____

Philippians 3:3 _____

Write a summary statement describing the work of the Holy Spirit in your life by paraphrasing 2 Corinthians 3:18.

_____

_____

THE POWER PACT

When you invited Christ into your life, it was the Holy Spirit who entered in. After you received Christ, your body became the temple of the Holy Spirit (1 Corinthians 3:16). You need to be willing to allow the Holy Spirit to operate within His temple.

Study and outline Romans 8:1-11, giving an explanation of what happens when the Holy Spirit fills you. Use this basic diagram to help you.

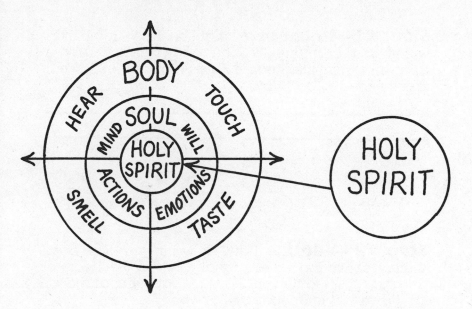

Why do you need to be filled with the Holy Spirit? Be specific.

_____

_____

Is anything in your life preventing you from being filled with the Holy Spirit?

_____

_____

The following steps will help you learn to be filled with the Holy Spirit *daily* so you will remain under His control. Pray through each step as you ask God to fill you with His Holy Spirit.

Step #1—Recognize that the Holy Spirit lives within you permanently because you have asked Christ into your life. Read 1 Corinthians 6:19-20. What do you need to do? Why?

_____

_____

Step #2—Realize that God wants you to be completely controlled by His Spirit. (This is the heart of allowing Jesus to be your Lord.) What command does God give you in Ephesians 4:17-18?

_____

_____

Step #3—Repent of any sin in your life. Do certain things in your life displease God? Jesus provided forgiveness and deliverance from sin on the cross. His forgiveness becomes real when you confess your sin to Him (agree with God about it). His promise to you in 1 John 1:9 will then become special to you. What sin(s) do you need to confess right now?

_____

Step #4—Renounce (abandon) *your* desires in order to follow *God's* desires. What does Galatians 2:20 teach about dealing with your desires?

_____

_____

What desires do you now control that you need to turn over to the Holy Spirit?

_____

_____

Step #5—Release the fullness of the Holy Spirit in you by faith. *Do it now.* Just as you received the Spirit of God into your life when you became a Christian, so receive the filling of the Spirit now by faith. What promise do you have from God about receiving the Holy Spirit? (Galatians 3:14)

_____

_____

Write a prayer here, asking God to release the Holy Spirit into your life.

_____

_____

_____

MAKING IT PERSONAL

Now that you understand how the Holy Spirit can change your life and give you more strength and power, let Him do that. Again, the Life Change sheet will examine just one area that most people need to change. As you think through your "habits," complete the study from Ephesians and answer all the questions.

Complete this Bible study by memorizing Ephesians 5:18.

ASSIGNMENT:
1. Have a time alone with God every day this week using the following Bible readings.
   Day 1: Mark 10:17-31
   Day 2: Mark 10:32-34
   Day 3: Mark 10:35-45
   Day 4: Mark 10:46-52
   Day 5: Mark 11:1-14
   Day 6: Mark 11:15-19
   Day 7: Mark 11:20-26
2. Complete *Bible study 8.*

LIFE CHANGE

ISSUE: Habits
BIBLE STUDY: Ephesians 5:1-18. Use the space below to record your comments.

My weaknesses in the area of habits are: _____

_____

_____

_____

My strengths in the area of habits are: _____

_____

_____

_____

ACTION POINT
From my study of Ephesians 5:1-18, I need to make
Jesus Lord of my habits by: _____

_____

_____

_____

I will take the following specific step of action to get rid
of my bad habits and replace them with habits that
honor God.

_____

_____ will pray with me about this.

NOTES

8

GET IN SHAPE!

Throwing off the hindrances

Last night we played our biggest rival, and I ran out of steam during the third quarter. I really feel like I let the team and the coach down. Monday I'm going to ask Coach how I can build up my endurance so I can finish stronger than I started.

Paul once challenged the Galatian church: "You were running a good race. Who cut in on you and kept you from obeying the truth?" (Galatians 5:7) The writer of Hebrews tells us to "throw off everything that hinders and the sin that so easily entangles, and let us run with perseverance the race marked out before us" (Hebrews 12:1).

What hinders us from running the race with endurance? Let's look at some common hindrances and then see how we can "throw them off."

HINDRANCES TO SERIOUS "RUNNERS"

A list of those hindrances is found in Galatians 5:19-21. Let's take one group at a time and see how they hinder Jesus' control of your life.

HINDRANCE #1—"SEXUAL IMMORALITY, IMPURITY, AND DEBAUCHERY"

These days it is pretty acceptable to participate in casual sexual relationships. If you are a virgin, you might even be an outcast (in the eyes of the people at school, that is). But what does God think about sexual purity? Read 1 Thessalonians 4:3-6. What should you avoid?

_____

_____

What do you need to do instead? Why?

_____

_____

Why is sex outside of marriage such a problem? When you don't wait for the proper person, time, and place (marriage), your focus is more on, "I need to gratify my sexual desires" than, "This is an expression of my love for you." You end up using the other person to fulfill your own selfish motives. By learning to control your sex life, you will be more able to respond with love and concern to the other person. A lack of control in this area indicates that sex is more important to you than Jesus is.

HINDRANCE #2—"IDOLATRY AND WITCHCRAFT"

Idolatry is giving ultimate worth to someone or something other than God. Some of our idols seem innocent enough. Others are obviously wrong. Below are three common idols you might be tempted by. (Of course, there are many, many more.)

Popularity—In school, recognition is the name of the game. The emphasis always seems to be on grades, elections, dating, or senior superlatives. What does Paul say about popularity? (Galatians 1:10)

_____

_____

Why is it wrong to put too much emphasis on trying to please others?

_____

_____

Pride—Egotistical pride makes you think you are more important than you really are. What does Peter encourage us to replace pride with? (1 Peter 5:5) Why?

The Occult—Do you read your horoscope often? Do you experiment with a Ouija board? What about "Dungeons and Dragons"? What warning are we given in Leviticus 19:31?

HINDRANCE #3—"HATRED, DISCORD, JEALOUSY, FITS OF RAGE, SELFISH AMBITION, DISSENTIONS, FACTIONS, AND ENVY"

These are all negative emotions that keep you from living in harmony with other people. Here are a couple of specific examples.

Bitterness—With all of the hurt that goes with broken homes and unfulfilled expectations, it's easy to see why students experience so much bitterness today. But bitterness eats away at you. Read Hebrews 12:15. What happens when we remain bitter over a period of time?

Envy and jealousy—Do you resent the accomplishments and prosperity of other people? You can find some good advice in Proverbs 14:30. Summarize that advice below. (Use *The Living Bible* if possible.)

HINDRANCE #4—"DRUNKENNESS, ORGIES, AND THE LIKE"

This set of hindrances refers to the "party spirit." You are probably familiar with the following symptoms.

Escapism—Drugs, alcohol, television, and even video games have become popular ways of escape, today more than ever. But people have tried to escape reality for centuries. Read Proverbs 23:29-35 to discover one popular way people tried to escape during Bible times. What method did they use?

_____

What are the results of trying to escape reality in that manner?

_____

_____

_____

Pleasure—The overwhelming desire for pleasure expresses itself in a lot of different ways: clothes, cars, stereos, trips, and so forth. A person who overemphasizes pleasure always has to manipulate his outward circumstances in order to be happy. What happens if you love pleasure too much? (Proverbs 21:17)

_____

_____

Selfishness is the bottom line for someone who puts pleasure above all else.

THROWING OFF YOUR HINDRANCES

What are the three biggest hindrances that interfere with your relationship with Jesus Christ?

_____

_____

What is the key to throwing off those hindrances that bog down your spiritual growth? (Galatians 5:16)

Before you can *run* a good race, you have to learn to *walk* by the Spirit.

In the last chapter, you learned how to be filled with the Spirit. But how do you "walk by the Spirit" every day?

STEP #1—BE FILLED CONTINUALLY WITH THE HOLY SPIRIT (EPHESIANS 5:18)

This happens when you allow Him to control or influence you totally. At first the Holy Spirit might bring to light an area of your life that needs to be changed. *Walking* in the Spirit takes place when you yield that area to the Lord day by day. You continue to allow the Holy Spirit to shed light on and change you in that area. Eventually, you ask Him to control your behavior *all the time*.

STEP #2—DO NOT QUENCH THE HOLY SPIRIT (1 THESSALONIANS 5:19)

What does it mean to "quench" the Holy Spirit? It's when you choose not to do what He directs you to do. For example, when you feel prompted by the Spirit to call a friend, but don't, you've quenched the Spirit. You can say no or ignore Him, but His prompting is always for your own good, or the good of others.

STEP #3—DO NOT GRIEVE THE HOLY SPIRIT (EPHESIANS 4:30)

The Holy Spirit is grieved whenever you deliberately choose to sin. For example, when you know it's not right to date a non-Christian, but choose to do it anyway, you grieve the Spirit. By doing so, you say yes to sin and no to God.

GETTING BACK ON TRACK

What do you do when you know you're no longer walking with the Spirit because you've quenched or grieved Him? You stay on track by learning to breathe spiritually. Physical breathing comes naturally for you. You've been breathing all the time you have been working on this chapter, but you haven't even noticed it. You exhale, ridding your lungs of all their carbon dioxide impurities. Then you inhale to take in the life-giving oxygen your body needs.

In a similar way, spiritual breathing keeps your spiritual life healthy. And after you practice it for a while, it will become like your physical breathing—a natural process.

You *exhale* by confessing. Confession means you get specific and identify the source(s) of whatever has caused the problem. Then you confess (agree with God) that you have quenched or grieved the Spirit.

You *inhale* by claiming two things: God's cleansing (1 John 1:9) and God's filling of the Holy Spirit (Ephesians 5:18). The great thing about breathing is that you can do it as often as you want or need to. If you are undergoing a particularly difficult ordeal, you will probably breathe a little harder than normal. Spiritual breathing works the same way, so don't hesitate to do it as often as you need to. God wants you to walk by the Spirit, so begin to practice your spiritual breathing exercises right away.

MAKING IT PERSONAL

Beginning to walk by the Spirit is the first step you can take toward getting in shape. Are you walking in the Spirit? To make this session really personal in your life, work through the Life Change sheet on "Temptation." Review Galatians 5:19-21 and specifically name some of the temptations that hinder you from walking with the Spirit.

Complete this Bible study by memorizing Galatians 5:16.

ASSIGNMENT:
1. Have a time alone with God every day this week using the following Bible readings:
   Day 1: Mark 11:27-33
   Day 2: Mark 12:1-12
   Day 3: Mark 12:13-27
   Day 4: Mark 12:28-34
   Day 5: Mark 12:35-40
   Day 6: Mark 12:41-44
   Day 7: Mark 13
2. Complete *Bible study 9.*

LIFE CHANGE

ISSUE: Temptation
BIBLE STUDY: James 1:2-4, 12-22. Use the space below
to record your comments.

_____

_____

_____

_____

_____

_____

_____

_____

_____

My weaknesses in the area of temptation are: _____

_____

_____

_____

My strengths in the area of temptation are: _____

_____

_____

_____

ACTION POINT
From my study of James 1:2-4, 12-22, I need to make
Jesus Lord over my temptations by: _____

_____

_____

_____

I will take the following specific step of action to prepare myself to overcome any temptation I face:

_____

_____ will pray with me about this.

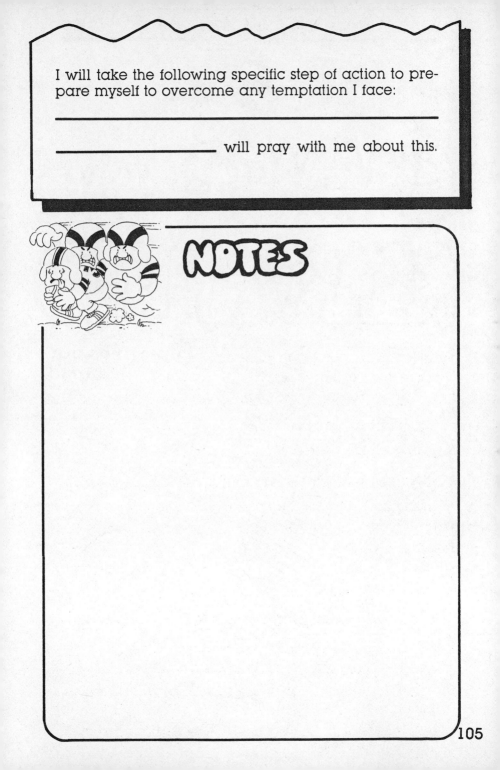

NOTES

9

CHANGED AND REARRANGED

Improving your thoughts

HIGH SCHOOL GAZETTE

TEAM MAKES PLAY-OFFS
9-2 RECORD

Now that we are moving toward the end of the season and the playoffs, I can look back and see how I've improved. I feel great, even though I also see a need to keep getting better. But what's next? When will I know I've "arrived"?

In making Jesus Lord, hopefully you have experienced similar feelings of "What's next?" or "When do I get this thing licked?" You have seen Jesus change many areas of your life, but you wonder, "How much more is He going to change?"

CHANGED STATUS

More changes occurred when you became a Christian than you may be aware of. You weren't just changed—you were totally rearranged! A verbal picture of how you were changed and rearranged is given in Romans 6:3-11.

Christ died (6:3).	Christ was buried (6:4).	Christ was raised from the dead (6:4).
When you received Christ, you died.	When you received Christ, you were buried.	When you received Christ, you were raised from the dead.

Repeat the following phrases twice to help them sink in:

- ⇨ Christ died, so I died.
- ⇨ Christ was buried, so I was buried.
- ⇨ Christ was raised from the dead, so I was raised from the dead.

According to Romans 6:4, you were raised to live a _____ life.

You may say, "I don't *feel* dead," or "I don't *feel* new!" On the first sunny day of summer you may not *feel* the sun burning your skin. But the next day you can both see and feel the change that has taken place.

Some things have to be recognized and accepted by faith—even though you can't feel, taste, or touch them. So here's how to act on your faith:

- ⇨ Know what God says about you (Romans 6:6, 9).
- ⇨ Count yourself as dead to sin and alive to God (Romans 6:11).
- ⇨ Yield youself to God (Romans 6:13).

As you grow and then look back, the reality of your new life is something that you can be sure of.

CHANGED THINKING

How much will you change? After you become a new person on the inside, you will begin to notice outer changes as well. The following chart lists some of those changes.

Before you became a Christian	After you became a Christian
You were dead in your transgressions and sins (Ephesians 2:1).	You became alive to God (Ephesians 2:5).
You were controlled by what *you* thought was right or wrong (Ephesians 2:3).	You are controlled by what *God* says is right and wrong (Ephesians 2:10).
You were a slave to sin (Romans 6:6).	You are a son of God (Galatians 4:7).

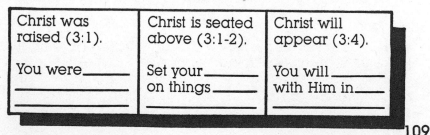

How does the new you on the inside become the new you on the outside too? As your old self (the one before you became a Christian), you learned how to think and act a certain way. But that old self died. Since you have become a Christian and received a new self, you can now begin to think and act differently. How? Study the following diagrams, and then fill in the missing words from Colossians 3:1-4:

Christ was raised (3:1).	Christ is seated above (3:1-2).	Christ will appear (3:4).
You were_____ _____	Set your_____ on things_____	You will_____ with Him in____

Now read Ephesians 4:22-24. In your own words, how will you be changed?

_____

_____

Many of your outward changes depend on your inner *mind-set*—learning to think a new way. The boxed quote breaks down the process for you.

> Sow a thought, reap an action.
> Sow an action, reap a habit.
> Sow a habit, reap a lifestyle.
> Sow a lifestyle, reap a destiny!

In other words, your thoughts determine your destiny. A.W. Tozer said, "The most important thing about you is what you think about Jesus, because what you think about Jesus will determine who you are and how you behave."

How can you begin to sow thoughts that will eventually reap a destiny of being "conformed to the likeness of His Son?" (Romans 8:29) Two ways: *putting off* and *putting on*.

PUTTING OFF

When you exercise, you sweat. When you sweat, your clothes begin to stink. If you're a slob, you might continue to wear your sweaty clothes for several days until they get really rank. But if you are a self-respecting person, you will take those clothes off, take a shower, and then put on some clean clothes.

You need to "put off" unclean thoughts just like you would put off rank, smelly, stinking clothes. Read Colossians 3:5-9. What are some of those thoughts that need to be put off?

_____

_____

_____

_____

List some of *your* thoughts that fall into the above categories. Be honest.

_____

_____

_____

_____

What happens if you decide *not* to put off those types of thoughts? Imagine you are a fish and you see an absolutely gorgeous worm dangling down in the water. You swim up to look at the worm. *Hmmmm*, you think, *it looks pretty good, but I'd better stay away. I've been told that there is usually a hook tied to a string which is tied to a pole at the end of that worm.*

You swim away, but you can't get that big, fat, juicy worm out of your mind. You keep imagining how good that worm would taste, so you swim back and look at it again. You think, *No, looks good but I'd better pass.* Yet you continue to swim around it and around it again—kind of checking out the situation.

The more you swim, the better that worm looks. You think, *I can just feel it going down my throat and how good it will taste.* Finally, *chomp*—you take the bait, you're hooked, and you're dead.

James 1:13-15 describes a similar process:

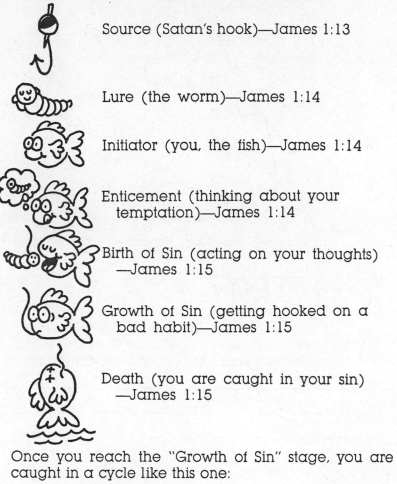

Source (Satan's hook)—James 1:13

Lure (the worm)—James 1:14

Initiator (you, the fish)—James 1:14

Enticement (thinking about your temptation)—James 1:14

Birth of Sin (acting on your thoughts) —James 1:15

Growth of Sin (getting hooked on a bad habit)—James 1:15

Death (you are caught in your sin) —James 1:15

Once you reach the "Growth of Sin" stage, you are caught in a cycle like this one:

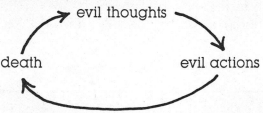

evil thoughts

evil actions

death

You can't control the source (Satan). Sometimes you can't even control the lure (bait) he tosses at you. But you *can* control your thoughts about it. "Set your minds on the things above, not on earthly things" (Colossians 3:2).

PUTTING ON

Read Colossians 3:12-17. As your mind is renewed, positive changes will take place in your life. Make a list of the qualities with which you should clothe yourself.

_____

_____

_____

_____

These changes will occur as you "think on these things." What things? Read Philippians 4:8 and list what you are to think about.

_____

_____

_____

_____

How can you learn to think on these things? Here are some practical suggestions.

STEP #1—DEVELOP A HABIT OF CONSCIOUSLY THINKING ABOUT YOUR LIFE IN CHRIST.

Repeat these statements each day:
- ⇨ "I am dead to myself" (Colossians 3:3).
- ⇨ "I am alive to Christ" (Romans 6:4).
- ⇨ "My life is hidden with Christ in God" (Colossians 3:3).
- ⇨ "Christ is *in* me" (Colossians 1:27).

STEP #2—MEMORIZE SCRIPTURE.

The practice of committing God's Word to memory will renew your mind. Write down some of the verses you have memorized word for word that help you keep your mind on "things above."

STEP #3—RESIST TEMPTATION.

Because you are a new creature in Christ, it should be very difficult for temptation to get to you.

Remember: Your life is hidden with Christ in God (Colossians 3:4). Think of yourself as protected from temptation without and within. If you are tempted, you have Jesus Christ living inside you. You are *dead* to sin (and dead men don't respond to temptation). You are *alive* to Christ, so let Jesus deal with any temptation you face.

So when you get up in the morning,
when some ungodly thought comes to mind,
when you are afraid, lonely, or pressured, or
when you have idle time...
THINK ON THESE THINGS.

MAKING IT PERSONAL

To make this session specific for you, select one area of your thought life (refer back to your list from Colossians 3:5-9) and work through the Life Change sheet.

Complete this Bible study by memorizing Colossians 3:1.

ASSIGNMENT:
1. Have a time alone with God every day this week using the following Bible readings.
   Day 1: Mark 14:1-2
   Day 2: Mark 14:3-9
   Day 3: Mark 14:10-11
   Day 4: Mark 14:12-16
   Day 5: Mark 14:17-21
   Day 6: Mark 14:22-26
   Day 7: Mark 14:27-31

2. Complete *Bible study 10.*

LIFE CHANGE

ISSUE: Thought Life
BIBLE STUDY: Philippians 4:8. Use the space below to record your comments.

_____

_____

_____

_____

_____

_____

_____

_____

_____

My weaknesses in the area of my thought life are: ___

_____

_____

_____

My strengths in the area of my thought life are: _____

_____

_____

_____

ACTION POINT
From my study of Philippians 4:8, I need to make Jesus
Lord of my thought life by: _____

_____

_____

I will take the following specific step of action to rid my
mind of unclean thoughts and "set my mind on things
above":

_____

_____

_____ will pray with me about this.

NOTES

10

WHO OWNS YOU?

**Making your
choice**

Today was the final game of the year. As I look back, it's encouraging to see how much I've improved. All of the hard work has really paid off. After the game, one of the college coaches offered me a scholarship to play next season. I'm really honored and excited, but I'm sure the demands will be even tougher.

Making Jesus Lord does not insure that your life will become easier. In fact, the challenges usually seem to get harder. But we have a promise as we move ahead: "My God will meet all your needs according to His glorious riches in Christ Jesus" (Philippians 4:19).

Making Jesus Lord is described in Matthew 13:44-46 in two parables. What parallels do you see between these parables and the opening illustration about accepting the scholarship?

_____

_____

_____

In order to get a clearer picture, think of making Jesus Lord this way: Jesus hands you a blank check in exchange for a blank sheet of paper. Let's examine that concept more closely.

A LIVING SACRIFICE

The blank check Jesus gives you represents everything you need to live life at its very best. Check out these verses to discover some of the promises included in Jesus' "blank check."

Romans 8:32 _____

Ephesians 1:3 _____

2 Peter 1:3 _____

In return for Christ's provisions, you need to give Him your life as a blank sheet of paper—with no restrictions. He can write on it whatever He desires for you. Romans 12:1-2 explains how the process works. Paul's first word is "Therefore," so he is referring back to what he had been saying in the earlier chapters of Romans. Basically he is saying that in light of this fantastic relationship that you have with God, and because of everything Jesus has done for you, you need to "offer your bodies as living sacrifices." What do you think that means?

_____

_____

When Paul says "offer your bodies," he means to put all of your mind, feelings, desires, and physical abilities at Jesus' disposal. He means you should offer yourself to God, just like animal sacrifices were put on the altar in the Old Testament.

How can you present your body on the altar? You have to make a willing choice to lay down your life and let God remove anything that competes with Jesus' desires for you. But Paul says you are to be a *living* sacrifice. What kind of living sacrifice are you to be? (Romans 12:1)

_____

_____

From your studies so far in *Making Jesus Lord,* what do you think it means to be a *living* sacrifice?

_____

_____

_____

Several suggestions on how you can present your body to Christ are given in Romans 12:9-21. What are some of them?

_____

_____

_____

_____

A CHANGED LIFE

When you make that big decision to "offer your body as a living sacrifice," then you can live every day "on the altar." As you learn to think of yourself as a sacrifice, you can know that Jesus is changing your life daily. How? Look at Romans 12:2. "Do not conform any longer to the pattern of this world" means you shouldn't try to be someone on the outside that you aren't on the inside. Have you ever caught yourself doing something you shouldn't or not doing something you should because of pressure from other people? How did you feel?

_____

_____

_____

"Be transformed by the renewing of your mind" means that you should begin to act on the outside like you already are on the inside. Your new life in Jesus Christ gives you the power to control all you do and say. What is one way that Jesus Christ is transforming your actions? Be specific.

_____

_____

Renewing your mind is the key to a changed life. If your thinking doesn't change, your actions won't either. Look back at the example you gave where you were doing or not doing something because of pressure from others. If you had concentrated on having Jesus Christ inside you, how might that situation have had different results?

_____

_____

The last part of Romans 12:2 ends by saying that "you will be able to test and approve what God's will is—His good, pleasing, and perfect will." After you have received the blank check of promises from Jesus and given Him your life as a blank sheet, you will be right in the middle of God's will and purpose for your life. The quality of your life in Christ will develop from "good" to "pleasing" to "perfect." It just gets better and better!

How is the Christian life getting better for you?

_____

_____

Why? _____

_____

GOD'S TROPHY

To bring everything together, look back to Romans 8:28-29. God promises to use *every* circumstance in your life for good when you are called according to His purpose (which you are). His purpose for you is "to be conformed to the likeness of His Son." In other words, you become like Him in everything you do.

The issues you have been working on throughout this book have helped you focus on some specific areas in your life that need to change. But those changes are already present *inside* you, because the Holy Spirit lives in you. Who are you compared to in 2 Corinthians 3:18?

_____

_____

The positive qualities that result from those inward changes will begin to be reflected in your behavior more and more as Jesus is Lord of your life.

Have you ever known anyone who was awarded a trophy? A trophy is special to its owner because it represents something the owner is proud of. When you make Jesus Lord of your life, you become God's trophy. Your life should reflect God to others. When they see you, they should also see something about Him.

A trophy belongs to the person who has his name on it, and that person can do whatever he wants with his trophy. Remember: you are God's trophy, and He owns you.

MAKING IT PERSONAL

Right now is a good time for you to be sure what Jesus is doing in your life. Sometimes the things He is working to change in us are different than what we want to change about ourselves. So take a few minutes and look back over the past ten weeks to see where *He* has been working. As you evaluate the Life Change sheets from the past eight weeks, take time to pray. Review each sheet and ask yourself: *What has God already done in this area?* Focus on the *Action Point* sections and determine any further action God might want you to take in each area. After you have finished reviewing all eight sheets, spend time in prayer and select the area that is most important for God to work on in your life *right now.*

TOPIC	WHAT GOD HAS ALREADY DONE	WHAT GOD IS LEADING ME TO DO NOW
Material Possessions		
Dating and Sex		
Friendships		
Parents		
Attitudes		
Habits		
Temptation		
Thought Life		

What specific area do you think is most in need of corrective action right now?

_____

What does God want you to do next?

_____

_____

Complete this Bible study by memorizing Romans 12:1-2.

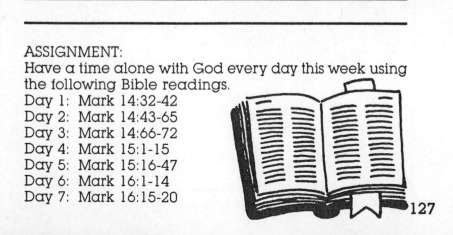

To close this study of *Making Jesus Lord,* spend a few minutes flipping back through each of the chapters to review what you studied. Then write in your own words what you feel you have learned about Jesus' lordship in your life. How has your commitment to Him changed since you began this study?

_____

_____

_____

ASSIGNMENT:
Have a time alone with God every day this week using the following Bible readings.
Day 1: Mark 14:32-42
Day 2: Mark 14:43-65
Day 3: Mark 14:66-72
Day 4: Mark 15:1-15
Day 5: Mark 15:16-47
Day 6: Mark 16:1-14
Day 7: Mark 16:15-20

NOTE: Even though you have completed this study of *Making Jesus Lord*, you will want to continue to spend time alone with God and memorize Scripture every day. You can get additional *Time Alone with God Notebook Inserts* at your local Christian bookstore, from the publisher of this book, or from Reach Out Ministries.

The next book in the Moving Toward Maturity series, *Giving Away Your Faith*, will help you learn how to share the life you have in Jesus Christ with others.